Written by
Trisha Callella

Editor: Sheri Samoiloff
Illustrator: Darcy Tom
Cover Illustrator: Tim Huhn
Designers: Moonhee Pak and Terri Lamadrid
Cover Designer: Barbara Peterson
Art Director: Tom Cochrane
Project Director: Carolea Williams

Table of Contents

Introduction

Do your students have trouble recognizing sight words? Do they make the same spelling mistakes over and over again in their writing? Do they pass their spelling test on Friday but misspell those same words when using them in a different context on Monday? *Making Your Word Wall More Interactive* helps resolve these problems. This resource guide targets a variety of skill areas and is designed to help students learn and REMEMBER new words in a fun and exciting way!

What Is a Word Wall?

A word wall is an organized collection of words written in large print and displayed in an area of the classroom where it can be easily seen. Designed to promote group learning, a word wall serves as a great classroom tool for individual students. It provides a rich context for active and ongoing learning that meets the needs of all students. A word wall is a constant work in progress as students practice and master each new set of words.

Why Use a Word Wall?

A word wall serves a variety of purposes, including the following:
- provides a visual for students that helps them remember connections between words
- serves as an important tool for helping students learn to read and spell new words
- fosters student independence
- promotes reading and writing
- holds students accountable for spelling specific words correctly at all times

This book features dozens of games and activities to engage students in literacy skill learning. So why wait? Let the games begin!

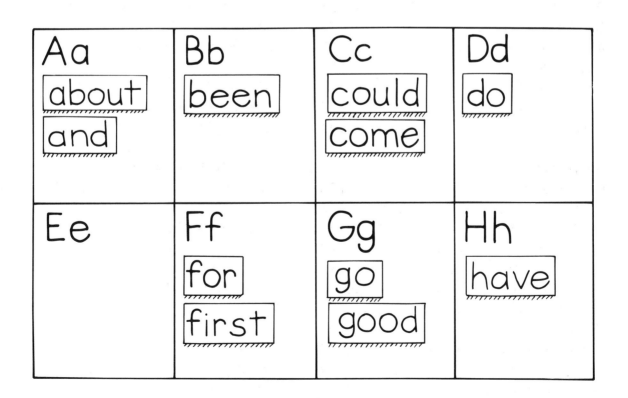

Getting Started

Before you implement the games and activities in this book, think about the organization and visual presentation of your word wall. Whether you already have a word wall in your classroom or you want to create one, consider the following questions:

• Is my word wall large enough to be viewed by all students from any part of the classroom?
• Is my word wall visually unified so that viewers will perceive it as a collection of words?
• Is it obvious how the words are organized?

Selecting a Style

Word walls come in many different shapes and sizes. Create a word wall that will complement your classroom setup, teaching style, and instructional goals. Many teachers choose to include the uppercase and lowercase version of each letter of the alphabet (e.g., *Aa*) on the word wall. Use premade die-cut letters, or cut letters out of construction paper. Here are just a few styles of word walls:

1. Display large letters in one row on a wall.
2. Glue each pair of die-cut letters (e.g., *Bb*) onto a separate piece of construction paper. Place the letters *Xx, Yy,* and *Zz* on the same piece of paper. Display the papers on a wall.

3. Use yarn to outline 24 squares on a wall. Place each pair of die-cut letters inside a separate square. Place the letters *Xx, Yy,* and *Zz* in the same square.

Choosing Words

It is important to begin with a blank word wall and add new words each week. Write the word wall words on colored paper, in large print, with black ink. The words can be cut in the shape of the letters, but it is not necessary. Avoid writing on red, dark purple, dark blue, or dark green construction paper because it is too hard for students to read the words. Tape the words onto your word wall rather than stapling them so they can be easily removed for use with some of the games and activities described in this book. Introduce approximately five words a week, depending on your grade level and the difficulty level of the words. Carry over to the following week any words students are still having difficulty spelling.

It is important to expose students to many different types of words. Use high-frequency words along with phonograms (word families), contractions, antonyms, synonyms, homophones, and other words to give your students an opportunity to become better at reading, spelling, and writing. Choose words wisely. It is better for students to know five words very well than ten words slightly. Add to the word wall any words several students misspell.

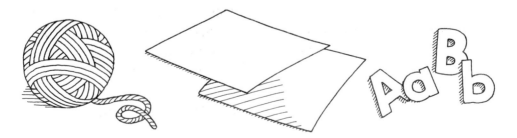

Preparation Tips

Many of the activities in this book require word cards and letter, word, or number dice. Here are some suggestions to minimize your preparation time:

Word Cards

- Give students blank index cards, and have them write the word wall words on the cards.
- Type word wall words in a large font size on a computer. Print several copies of the words on colored paper (to make sure the words do not show through). Cut the papers into word cards.
- Recycle the word cards for each activity. Add or eliminate words as needed.

Dice

- Invite students to assemble the dice.
- Recycle the dice for use with additional activities.

Covering the Word Wall

- Some activities suggest covering the word wall with butcher paper. It is important to make sure students are unable to see the words on the wall. An alternative is to have students face away from the word wall.

Word Wall Variations

There are many variations in the types of word walls that you can use with your students. Some word walls focus on a particular theme or content area. Others focus on parts or types of words. Use various types of word walls to teach students different ways to analyze words. Try some of the following variations once students are familiar with your classroom word wall.

Library Pocket Word Wall

Write each letter of the alphabet on a separate library pocket, and place the pockets in alphabetical order along the bottom of your word wall. Each time you add a new word to the word wall, write it on an index card, and place the card in the corresponding library pocket. Invite students to choose the cards they need and return them to the pockets when they are finished. This will be extremely helpful for students who are kinesthetic learners. (The word cards you create for this type of word wall can also be used in many of the games and activities in this book.)

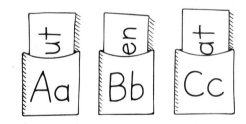

Phonogram Word Wall

Create a separate word wall for the letters *a, e, i, o,* and *u.* Write each new phonogram on an index card, and place each card under the appropriate vowel.

Individual Word Wall

Give each student the My Portable Word Wall reproducibles (pages 89–90). Have students place the reproducibles in their student writing journals. When you add a new word to the classroom word wall, invite students to write it on their portable word wall. This is a helpful resource for students to have when they write outside the classroom.

Using This Book

This book is divided into four sections. The first three sections feature whole-class, small-group, and independent games and activities. Use them in any order, and repeat them throughout the year with new words. The fourth section provides a variety of supplemental materials to help you get the most out of your word wall activities.

Whole Class

Use the interactive whole-class activities in the first section to teach language concepts and reinforce learning word wall words. Start with this section to familiarize students with the organization and purpose of the word wall.

Small Group

The second section includes interactive small-group activities that are designed to have students practice some of the same strategies, skills, and activities that are presented in the whole-class section. After introducing a small-group activity, students will be able to work independently. These activities work well in learning centers, and students can complete them every week.

Independent

Have students complete the open-ended reproducibles in the third section as independent activities. Or, use them for additional teaching opportunities or for guided practice with small groups of students who need extra help. These activities also work well as a follow-up to the whole-class and small-group lessons. The activities are presented in order by increasing levels of difficulty. Begin with the first few activities in this section, regardless of your students' ability level, and then use the independent activities as they pertain to what you are teaching.

Additional Resources

The fourth section includes a variety of reproducibles and word lists. Have students complete the Word Wall Spelling Quiz reproducible (page 88), and use it to track their progress. Use the results to determine which words to target with individual students in small-group activities. Use the lists of high-frequency words, compound words, antonyms, synonyms, phonograms, and homophones (pages 91–96) as a handy resource for developing new word wall words.

Get Moving

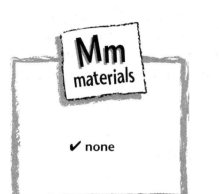

Mm
materials

✔ none

Pp
preparation

✔ none

Explain to the class that "tall letters" go from the top line to the bottom line on the paper (e.g., *d*). Tell students to put their arms in the air when they see these letters. Explain that "small letters" go from the dotted middle line to the bottom line (e.g., *a*). Ask them to put their arms straight out when they see these letters. Explain that "dropped letters" drop below the line (e.g., *y*). Ask students to squat when they see these letters. Invite one student to choose five to ten favorite word wall words. Ask the student to point to a word. Invite the class to say the word, "spell" it with the movements, and then say it again. Have the class repeat the activity with the rest of the student's words.

Vv
variation

Invite a student to choose a word from the word wall and, without saying the word aloud, demonstrate the movements of the word. Encourage the other students to guess the word.

The Missing Word

Mm materials

✔ none

As a class, read aloud the words on the word wall. Ask students to close their eyes as you remove one word from the word wall. Have them open their eyes and try to identify the missing word. Ask students to whisper the word and its spelling to a classmate. If they are having difficulty identifying the word, give location clues such as *The word is in the top row of the word wall* or *The word belongs somewhere between Aa and Ee.* Repeat the activity using different words from the word wall.

Pp preparation

✔ none

Vv variation

Use a large envelope to make a "sleeve" to cover the word card. Place the word card into the sleeve. Slowly slide the card out of the sleeve, showing one letter at a time. Have students spell the word as you pull it out.

8

All Mixed-Up

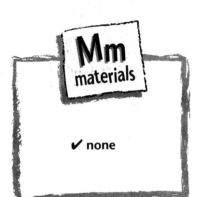

Mm materials

✔ none

Pp preparation

✔ none

As a class, read aloud the words on the word wall. Ask students to close their eyes while you remove five words and place them under the wrong letters. Have students open their eyes and look for the misplaced words. Give students time to think, and then ask them to whisper to a classmate which words are misplaced. Invite the class to say and spell one misplaced word at a time and tell which letter it belongs under. Move each word back to the correct letter. Repeat this process with the remaining misplaced words.

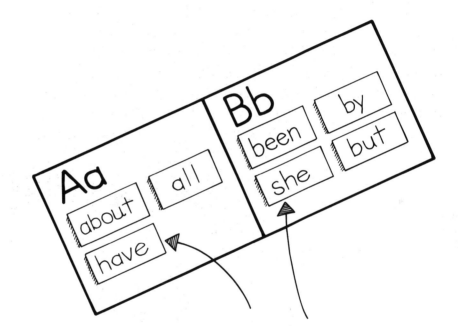

Vv variation

Have students complete this activity at their seats with an individual dry erase board or a piece of paper. Ask them to write down all the misplaced words and which letters they should go under. Have more advanced students write down the misplaced words and list all the words on the word wall that begin with the same letter. Invite students to put these words in alphabetical order.

Riddles, Riddles, Riddles

Mm
materials

✔ none

Pp
preparation

✔ none

Explain to the class that a riddle is a puzzling question posed as a problem to be solved or guessed. Tell students that they will each create their own riddle as a clue to a word from the word wall (e.g., *What has three letters, rhymes with rat, and starts with the letter c?*). Model a "think aloud" to help students learn how to create a riddle. For example, say *First I will choose a word in my head. Now I will try to think of challenging clues to make you think. I'm thinking of a word that has three tall letters,* and so on. The clues could include the number of letters in the word, a word that rhymes with the word wall word, a range of letters it is located between (e.g., between *c* and *f*), the number of vowels or consonants it has, the number of tall or dropped letters it has, or the row in which the word can be found on the word wall. Invite students to take turns sharing their riddle.

Vv
variation

Invite each student to write a riddle that uses a word from the word wall. Combine the students' riddles into a class riddle book.

Secret Letter Bag

Mm
materials

✔ letter cards
   (pages 12–13)
✔ scissors
✔ small bag

Pp
preparation

✔ Copy and cut apart
   the letter cards.
✔ Remove the
   duplicate cards.
✔ Place the cards
   in a bag.
✔ Place the bag next
   to the word wall.

Have a student reach into the "Secret Letter Bag" without looking and pull out two cards. Invite the student to show the rest of the class the letters. Ask the class which of the two letters comes first in the alphabet, and have the student hold the letters in that order. Explain to the class that this is the range from which they will be reading the word wall words. For example, if the letters are *b* and *h*, students will read all the words that begin with *b, c, d, e, f, g,* and *h*. To limit the number of words to be read, place a small range of letters in the bag (e.g., *a–d, f–h*).

Vv
variation

Create a picture card for each letter of the alphabet (e.g., an apple for *a*, a ball for *b*). Invite a student to choose two letter cards from the Secret Letter Bag. Discuss *range* and attach two pictures to your word wall to show the beginning and the end of the range of letters chosen. For example, if a student pulls out the letters *c* and *g*, place a picture of a cat and a goldfish on the word wall.

Letter Cards

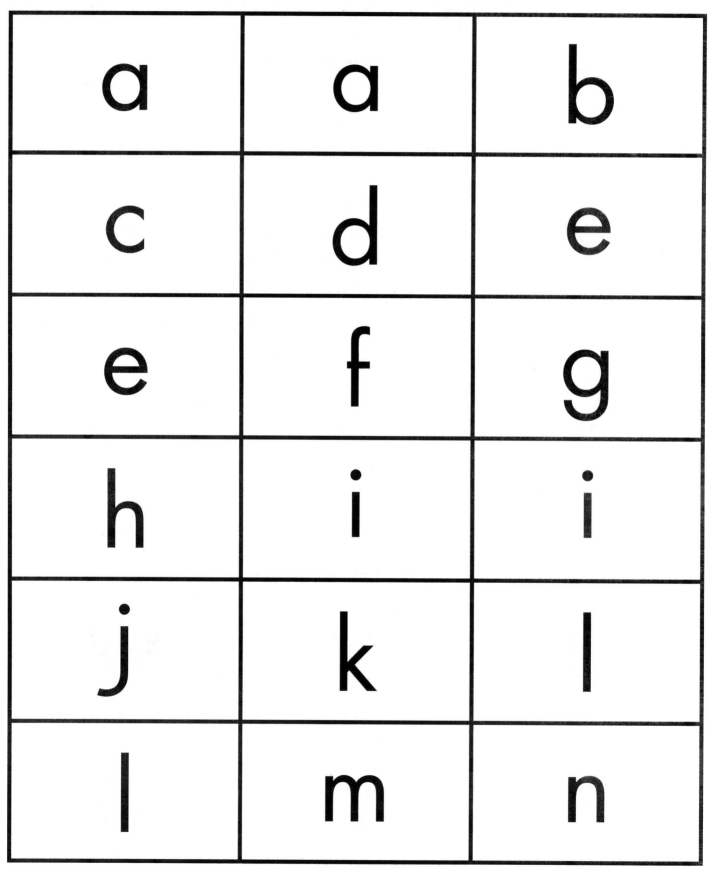

a	a	b
c	d	e
e	f	g
h	i	i
j	k	l
l	m	n

Making Your Word Wall More Interactive © 2001 Creative Teaching Press

Letter Cards

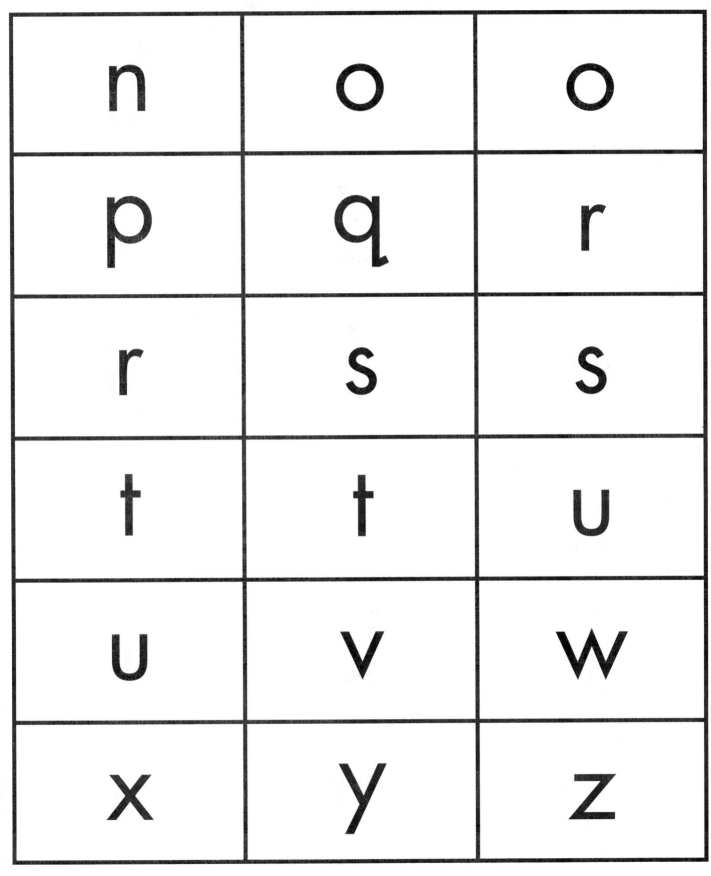

n	o	o
p	q	r
r	s	s
t	t	u
u	v	w
x	y	z

Person of the Day

Select a student to be the "Person of the Day." Have that student write his or her first name on the chalkboard. For younger students, tape a yellow happy face or die-cut next to each letter of the student's name on the word wall. This will make it easier for students to identify the letters. Ask the class to say each letter of the student's name and read all of the words on the word wall that begin with the same letters. Have students pair up with a partner and take turns spelling those words.

Mm
materials

✔ tape
✔ yellow happy faces or other die-cuts

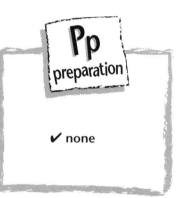

Pp
preparation

✔ none

Vv
variation

Invite a student to write his or her last name on the board.

Roll That Die

Have a student stand at the front of the classroom and roll the die. Have the student announce what numeral is showing. Point to the words on the word wall that have the same number of letters as the number rolled. For example, if a student rolls a 5, point to the words *house* and *three*. Invite students to say and spell these words. Ask students to count the number of words they spelled.

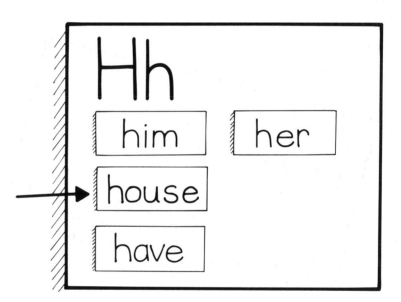

Mm materials

✔ Die pattern (page 16)
✔ paper or card stock
✔ scissors
✔ glue

Pp preparation

✔ Copy the Die pattern onto paper or card stock.
✔ Number the die from 3 to 8.
✔ Assemble the die.

Vv variation

Have students write these words on a piece of paper or dry erase board.

Die

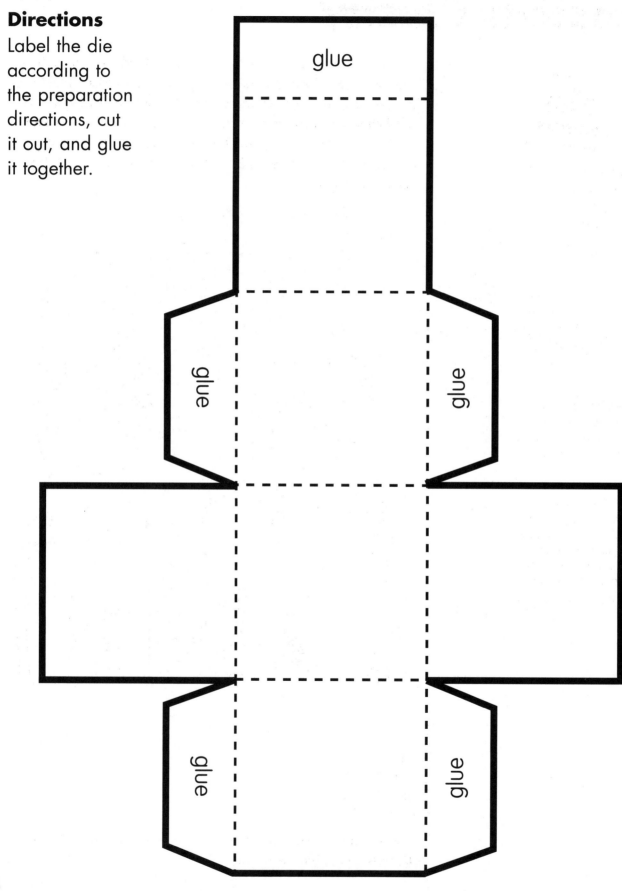

Making Your Word Wall More Interactive © 2001 Creative Teaching Press

Musical Chairs

Mm
materials

✔ index cards
✔ chairs
✔ music/cassette
  or CD player

Pp
preparation

✔ Write various
  word wall words
  on separate index
  cards. Make at
  least one card
  for each student.
✔ Arrange student
  chairs in pairs in a
  circle or row. Leave
  space between
  each set of chairs.
✔ Place one word
  card on each chair.

Play music, and invite students to walk around the chairs. Stop the music, and have each student pick up the word card from the nearest empty chair and sit down. Have students say and spell their word to the person sitting next to them. Ask students to stand up and place their word card back on the chair. Repeat the activity. Do not remove any chairs for this version of the game.

Vv
variation

Invite students to read their word card to a partner and have the partner spell the word.

17

Word Wall Toss

Select one student to be the "tosser." Invite this student to stand near the word wall and gently toss a ball at it. Have the class announce the letter that was hit. Ask students to read and spell aloud each word on the word wall that begins with that letter. For example, if the ball hits the letter *h*, the class says *h* and reads all the *h* words. Select another student to stand facing away from the word wall and try to recall all the words that begin with the selected letter. Continue to invite different students to recall the words until a student is able to remember all the words. To make this activity more challenging, invite the student to spell the words as well.

Mm
materials

✔ small "soft" ball

Pp
preparation

✔ none

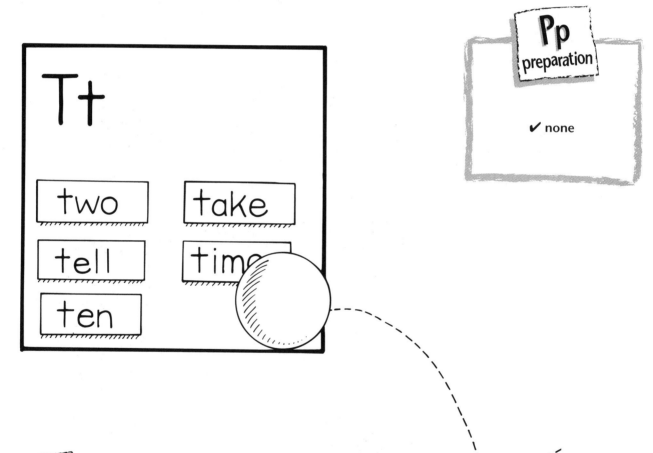

Vv
variation

Remove all of the words under the letter that was hit, and give an impromptu spelling quiz.

The Eraser Game

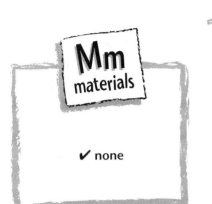

Mm
materials

✔ none

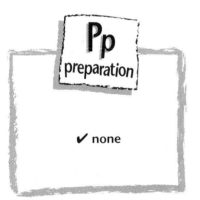

Pp
preparation

✔ none

W rite eight word wall words on the chalkboard. As you write each letter of a word, have the class predict what the word will be. After writing each word, have the class read the words written so far. Once all eight words are on the board, have the class close their eyes while you erase one word. Ask the class to open their eyes and try to identify which word you erased. Give students time to think before letting the class announce the word. Repeat the activity with the remaining words.

Vv
variation

Once you have erased all eight words, ask a student to name one of the selected words. Have the class spell this word as you write it again on the board. Repeat the activity with the rest of the words.

Spelling Circle

nvite the class to sit in a circle. Choose a student to think of a word from the word wall and tell the class the word. If the student can't think of a word, give him or her a clue or have another student whisper a word to the student. Have the next student in the circle say the first letter of the word. Ask students to continue spelling the word letter by letter. Invite the student who says the last letter to announce the word again. Repeat the game by asking the next student to choose a new word and announce it to the class. Allow a student to skip a turn if he or she is struggling to spell a word.

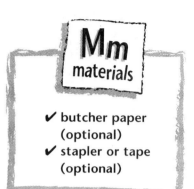

Mm
materials

✔ butcher paper (optional)
✔ stapler or tape (optional)

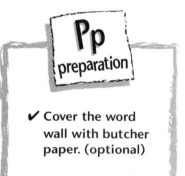

Pp
preparation

✔ Cover the word wall with butcher paper. (optional)

Vv
variation

Invite a student to think of a word with the same phonogram as a word on the word wall. For example, a student could say the word *trail* to correspond with the word wall word *pail*. Have students spell the word letter by letter.

Table Toss

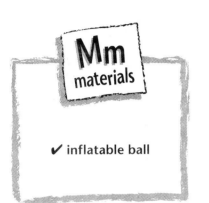

Mm
materials

✔ inflatable ball

nvite students to sit or stand at their desk or table. Give an inflatable ball to a student. Have that student say a word from the word wall and gently toss the ball to another student. Ask the student who caught the ball to spell the word, say a new word, and then gently toss the ball to another classmate. Continue the game until all students have had the opportunity to catch the ball and then say a new word.

Pp
preparation

✔ Before having students play this game, establish the following expectations:
   1. Students may talk only when they have the ball.
   2. Everyone must be at their desk at all times.
   3. The ball needs to be thrown gently.
   4. Everyone gets a chance to catch the ball.
   5. The ball cannot be thrown back to the person who threw it.

beside

Vv
variation

Have the student who tosses the ball spell a word. Invite the student who catches the ball to say the word and then spell a different word before tossing the ball to another student.

Pick a Partner

R andomly pass out one word card to each student. Explain to the class that they are to search for the classmate with their matching word. Have students repeatedly spell their word out loud while they search for their match. Invite partners to stand together in the back of the room. When all students have found their partner, invite each pair of students to go to the front of the room and spell their word for the class. Have the rest of the class say the word.

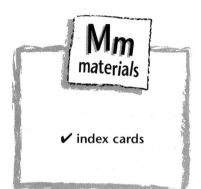

Mm
materials

✔ index cards

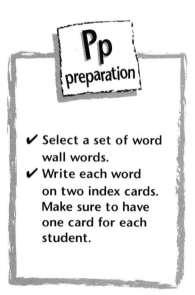

Pp
preparation

✔ Select a set of word wall words.
✔ Write each word on two index cards. Make sure to have one card for each student.

Vv
variation

Create word cards for a different type of word (e.g., compound words).

Word Wall Lotto

Mm
materials

✔ Word Wall Lotto
reproducible (page 24)
✔ counters (e.g.,
cubes, beans)

Pp
preparation

✔ Copy a class set of
the reproducible.

Give each student a reproducible and a handful of counters. Display 16 word wall words, and have students randomly write a word in each box on their sheet. Explain that the object of the game is to be the first player to cover four words in a row (horizontally, vertically, or diagonally). Call out one of the words. Invite students to find the word on their sheet and place a counter in that box. Continue calling out words until a student wins the game.

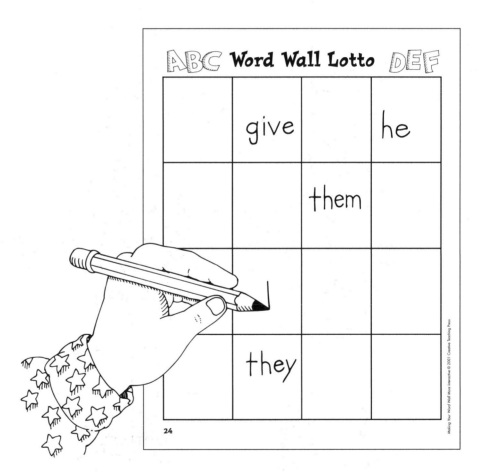

ABC **Word Wall Lotto** DEF

give | | he
| them |
| |
they | |

24

Vv
variation

Give students clues about each word (e.g., *The word has two vowels and three consonants*). Have them identify the word and cover it on their sheet.

23

ABC Word Wall Lotto DEF

Making Your Word Wall More Interactive © 2001 Creative Teaching Press

Word Wall Memory

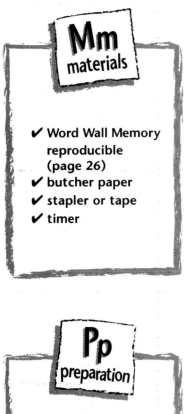

Mm materials

✔ Word Wall Memory reproducible (page 26)
✔ butcher paper
✔ stapler or tape
✔ timer

Pp preparation

✔ Copy the reproducible for each team of students.

Invite students to read the words on the word wall. Cover the word wall with butcher paper, and divide the class into teams of three to five students. Give each team a reproducible. Explain that team members are to work together to write on the reproducible at least one word from the word wall for every letter of the alphabet. Set a timer for 10 minutes. When time is up, uncover the word wall and have team members check the spelling of their words. Have teams award themselves one point for every word they correctly spelled. Give teams a free point for every letter on the word wall without any words. The team with the most points wins the game. Invite each team to read their list of words to the class and share how each team member contributed to the activity.

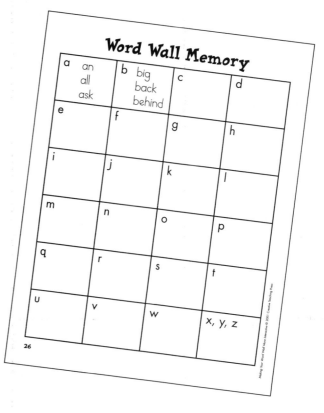

Vv variation

For each word wall word, have teams write a word from the same word family.

Word Wall Memory

a	b	c	d
e	f	g	h
i	j	k	l
m	n	o	p
q	r	s	t
u	v	w	x, y, z

What's My Word?

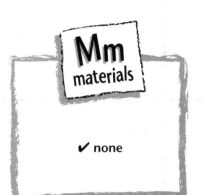

Mm
materials

✔ none

I nvite the class to sit in a circle. Have a student choose any word from the word wall and say it to the class. Ask the next student in the circle to try and spell the word. Ask the following student to say a different word from the word wall. Invite the next student to spell the word. Repeat the activity until every student has had a chance to say and spell one word from the word wall. If a student has trouble spelling a word, invite a classmate to point to the word on the word wall while the student spells it.

Pp
preparation

✔ none

Vv
variation

Invite the first student to spell a word. Have the next student say the word. Repeat the activity until every student has had a chance to spell and say two words.

27

Say the Magic Word

ivide the class into two teams. Have each team member sit behind one another, creating two single-file lines facing the chalkboard. Explain that the goal of the game is to be the first player to guess the word you slowly write on the board. The student who guesses the word first earns a team point and gets to finish spelling the rest of the word. Invite the first student on each team to stand facing the board. Choose any word from the word wall, and begin to write it on the board while the opponents try to guess the word. Encourage the other students to also try to guess the word but not say it aloud. Once a student has guessed and spelled the word, invite the class to repeat the spelling of the word. Have both students go to the end of the line. Invite the next pair of students to guess a different word. Play the game until all students have had a turn. The team with the most points at the end of the game wins. For struggling learners, match students up with an opponent with a similar ability level and choose a word that they can spell successfully.

Mm
materials

✔ none

Pp
preparation

✔ none

Vv
variation

Invite the student who guesses the correct word to select the next word and write it on the board for the other students to guess.

Alphabetize Me

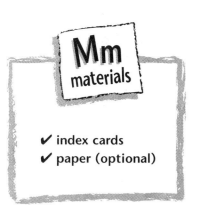

Mm
materials

✔ index cards
✔ paper (optional)

Pp
preparation

✔ Write a class set of word wall words on separate index cards.
✔ Write each letter of the alphabet on a separate piece of paper. (optional)

Randomly pass out one word card to each student. Have students arrange themselves in alphabetical order according to their word. Then, have students say and spell their word to the class. Collect the cards, shuffle them, and pass them out a second time. Have students repeat the activity with their new word. To extend the activity, divide the class into three or four groups and have students get into alphabetical order in their groups.

For younger students, write each letter of the alphabet on a separate piece of paper and place the papers on the floor in alphabetical order. For the word cards, if possible, write only one word for each letter of the alphabet. This will make it easier for students to get in the correct order. Pass out the cards, and have students find the piece of paper with the letter that matches the first letter of their word.

Vv
variation

Have students say their words in alphabetical order while the class spells the words together.

Word Wall Walk

ive each student a piece of paper or a notepad and a pencil. Have each student begin by standing on a card or paper. Play music, and invite students to walk from one card or paper to the next. Stop the music, and invite students to read the word they land on and record it on their piece of paper or notepad. Repeat the activity until each student has a list of ten words. Encourage students to take turns reading their list of words to a partner and challenging their partner to spell each word.

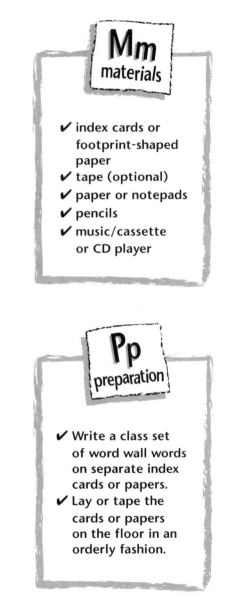

Mm
materials

✔ index cards or footprint-shaped paper
✔ tape (optional)
✔ paper or notepads
✔ pencils
✔ music/cassette or CD player

Pp
preparation

✔ Write a class set of word wall words on separate index cards or papers.
✔ Lay or tape the cards or papers on the floor in an orderly fashion.

Vv
variation

Ask students to pick a different partner, and have them quiz each other using the words they recorded during the walk.

Doorway Drill

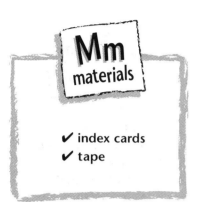

Mm materials

✔ index cards
✔ tape

Invite one student to choose five word cards and read them to the class. Have the class say the words together. Tape the words on the classroom door, and explain that whenever students leave the room they must quietly read and spell the displayed words. When the entire class leaves the classroom, have students say the words to a partner and have the partners spell the words. Repeat this activity every day with different word cards.

Pp preparation

✔ Write 30 word wall words on separate index cards.

Vv variation

Use an overhead marker to write the five words of the day on a laminated hall pass. Encourage students to read the words when they are outside of the classroom, and randomly ask students to spell the words as they walk back into the classroom.

Four in a Row

ivide the class into five teams, and assign each team a color or shape. Explain that the object of the game is to be the first team to get four counters in a row (horizontally, vertically, or diagonally) while blocking the other teams from doing the same. Tell them each team earns a counter by correctly spelling a word wall word. Display the transparency. Say a word wall word, and have one student from the first team spell it. If the student spells it correctly, have the team discuss where to put their counter on the grid. Continue the game until one team wins.

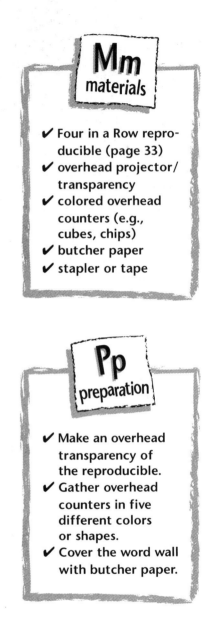

Mm materials

✔ Four in a Row repro-
  ducible (page 33)
✔ overhead projector/
  transparency
✔ colored overhead
  counters (e.g.,
  cubes, chips)
✔ butcher paper
✔ stapler or tape

Pp preparation

✔ Make an overhead
  transparency of
  the reproducible.
✔ Gather overhead
  counters in five
  different colors
  or shapes.
✔ Cover the word wall
  with butcher paper.

Vv variation

Divide the class into teams of four students. Give each team a reproducible and counters. Give each student a piece of scratch paper. Have each team play against another team. Encourage students to record the correctly spelled words on their own piece of paper.

Four in a Row

Make My Word

ive each student a bag or envelope of letter cards. Say a word wall word, and invite students to use their letter cards to spell the word on their desk. Have students check a classmate's spelling of the word, and then spell the word together. Repeat the activity with different word wall words. To extend the activity, invite a student to select a word wall word and say it to the class. Encourage the class to spell the word with their letter cards. For more advanced students, copy two sets of the letter cards. This will allow students to make larger words.

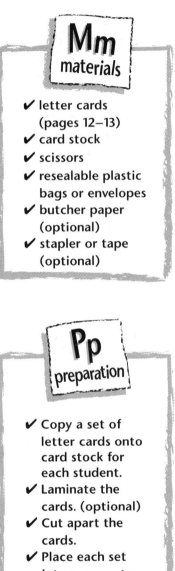

Mm
materials

✔ letter cards
  (pages 12–13)
✔ card stock
✔ scissors
✔ resealable plastic
  bags or envelopes
✔ butcher paper
  (optional)
✔ stapler or tape
  (optional)

Pp
preparation

✔ Copy a set of
  letter cards onto
  card stock for
  each student.
✔ Laminate the
  cards. (optional)
✔ Cut apart the
  cards.
✔ Place each set
  into a separate
  bag or envelope.
✔ Cover the word
  wall with butcher
  paper. (optional)

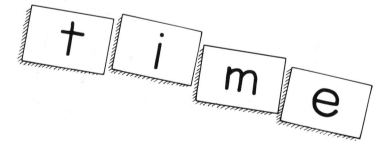

Vv
variation

Give clues to a secret word wall word. Encourage students to combine the clues to identify the word. Have them use the letter cards to spell the word.

Partner Quiz

Mm
materials

✔ letter cards
  (pages 12–13)
✔ scissors

Randomly give one letter card to each student. Have students work in pairs. Explain to the class that they will quiz their partner on all of the word wall words that begin with the letter they have. For example, if one student has the *m* card, his or her partner would read all the words on the word wall that begin with *m* (one at a time) and ask the student to spell each word without looking at the word wall. Then, have partners switch roles and repeat the activity.

Pp
preparation

✔ Copy and cut apart the letter cards.

Vv
variation

Give two letter cards to each student. Have students repeat the activity with both letters and record the words they spell in a spelling journal.

Flip It Down!

ivide the class into teams of two to four players. Give each player a copy of the reproducible, and give each team two dice. Explain that the object of the game is to be the first player on a team to "flip down" all the words on his or her game board. Begin the game by having the first player on each team roll the dice. Invite him or her to read the words that are facing up on the dice and flip down the matching words on his or her game board. If players roll a word they have already flipped, they lose their turn. Have players continue to play the game until a player on each team has flipped down all the words.

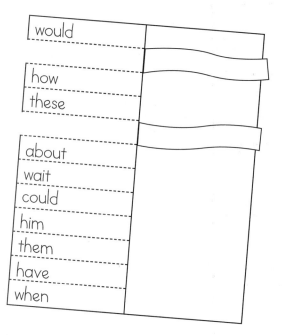

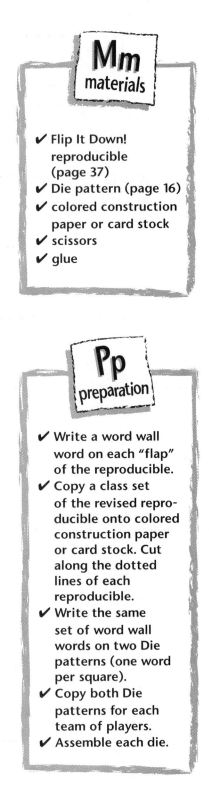

Mm
materials

✔ Flip It Down! reproducible (page 37)
✔ Die pattern (page 16)
✔ colored construction paper or card stock
✔ scissors
✔ glue

Pp
preparation

✔ Write a word wall word on each "flap" of the reproducible.
✔ Copy a class set of the revised reproducible onto colored construction paper or card stock. Cut along the dotted lines of each reproducible.
✔ Write the same set of word wall words on two Die patterns (one word per square).
✔ Copy both Die patterns for each team of players.
✔ Assemble each die.

Vv
variation

Give each student a blank reproducible, and give each team two blank Die patterns. Ask each team of students to choose word wall words and write them on their reproducible and on the Die patterns. Have students cut along the dotted lines of their reproducible and assemble the dice. Invite students to flip down the words on their reproducible as they roll the words. The first student to flip down all the words wins the game.

Flip It Down!

Tic-Tac-Toe! Three Words in a Row!

Have students work in pairs. Give each pair a reproducible, a set of word cards, and two different types of counters. Have pairs place the cards facedown in a pile. Explain that this game is similar to Tic-Tac-Toe, except students must spell a word wall word correctly before they place a counter on a square. For example, player A picks up the top card and reads the word to player B. If player B correctly spells the word, he or she places a counter on any open square of the game board. If player B gives an incorrect response, player A correctly spells the word and places the word card at the bottom of the pile and player B's turn is over. The players continue to take turns reading and spelling words. The first player to place three counters in a row (horizontally, vertically, or diagonally) wins the game.

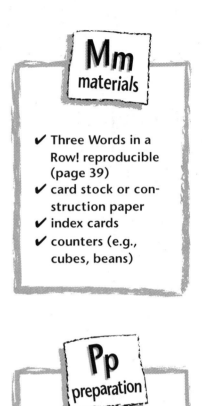

Mm
materials

✔ Three Words in a
Row! reproducible
(page 39)
✔ card stock or con-
struction paper
✔ index cards
✔ counters (e.g.,
cubes, beans)

Pp
preparation

For each pair
of students:
✔ Copy the
reproducible
onto card stock
or construction
paper.
✔ Laminate the
reproducible.
(optional)
✔ Write 20 word
wall words on
separate index
cards.

Vv
variation

Invite students to spell the word on the card instead of reading it. Explain that the opponent must say the word before placing a counter on the game board.

Three Words in a Row!

Roll Twenty

ivide the class into teams of two to four players. Give each team a reproducible, a die, and a set of word cards. Have teams place the cards facedown in a pile. Explain that the goal of the game is to be the first player on a team to spell 20 word wall words. Have each team member write his or her name at the top of a column on the reproducible. Ask the first player to roll the die. Have the second player read that number of word cards to the first player, who tries to spell each word. Tell the first player to record each word he or she spelled correctly in his or her column of the reproducible. Have students place the word cards facedown at the bottom of the pile at the end of each player's turn. Ask students to continue rolling the die and spelling words until one player has spelled 20 words.

Mm
materials

✔ Roll Twenty reproducible (page 41)
✔ index cards
✔ dice

Pp
preparation

For each team of players:
✔ Copy the reproducible.
✔ Write 20–30 word wall words on separate index cards.

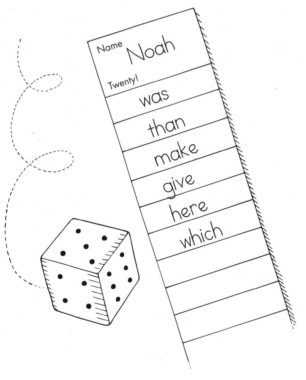

Name	Noah
Twenty!	
	was
	than
	make
	give
	here
	which

Vv
variation

Have each team of students write any 20 word wall words on separate index cards and use them to play the game again. When the teams are finished playing, have students exchange cards with another team and play again.

40

Roll Twenty

Name	Name	Name	Name
Twenty!	Twenty!	Twenty!	Twenty!

Speedy Spellers

Divide the class into teams of three players. Give each team a timer, a set of word cards, and a piece of scratch paper. Explain that the object of the game is to spell as many words as possible in one minute. Have teams start their timer. Invite the first player to read one word card at a time, while the second player tries to spell each word, and the third player tallies the number of correctly spelled words on the paper. After the first player's time is finished, have teams reset their timer and shuffle their cards. Have students continue to take turns reading, spelling, and tallying their answers. After each member of the team has had a chance to spell all the words, have the students count their points. The student with the most points wins the game. Give students a chance to improve their scores by allowing them to have a second try at spelling the words.

Mm
materials

✔ index cards
✔ minute timers
✔ scratch paper

Pp
preparation

✔ Write 20 word wall words on separate index cards for each team of players.

Vv
variation

Invite students to read the words on the cards instead of spelling them.

42

Catch My Fish

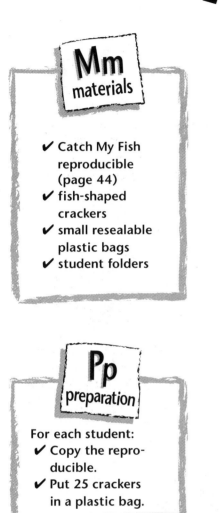

Mm materials

✔ Catch My Fish reproducible (page 44)
✔ fish-shaped crackers
✔ small resealable plastic bags
✔ student folders

Pp preparation

For each student:
✔ Copy the reproducible.
✔ Put 25 crackers in a plastic bag.

Give each student a reproducible and a bag of crackers. Have students write a different word from the word wall in each box on the reproducible. Have students work in pairs. Ask them to place a fish cracker in each box. Explain that player A will name a coordinate (e.g., *B5*). Player B will read the word in that box and ask player A to spell it. If player A correctly spells the word, he or she is given the cracker from the selected box on player B's reproducible. Have students continue to take turns picking coordinates and spelling words. Encourage students to use a folder as a divider to keep their grid hidden from their opponent. The first student to catch all of his or her opponent's fish wins the game.

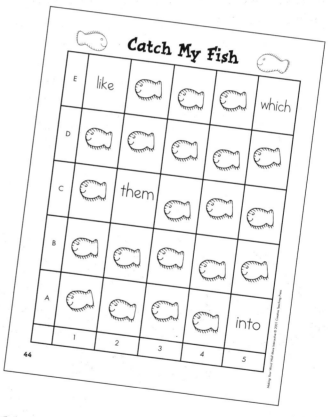

Vv variation

Have students use words with the same phonogram as words from the word wall.

 # Catch My Fish

E					
D					
C					
B					
A					
	1	2	3	4	5

Fruity Checkers

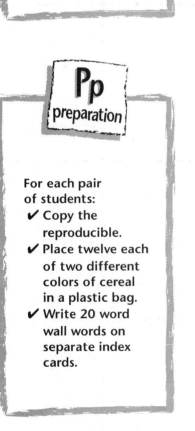

Mm
materials

✔ Fruity Checkers
   reproducible
   (page 46)
✔ fruit ring cereal
✔ small resealable
   plastic bags
✔ index cards

Pp
preparation

For each pair
of students:
✔ Copy the
   reproducible.
✔ Place twelve each
   of two different
   colors of cereal
   in a plastic bag.
✔ Write 20 word
   wall words on
   separate index
   cards.

Have students work in pairs. Give each pair a reproducible, a bag of cereal, and a set of word cards. Have pairs place the cards facedown in a pile. Invite each partner to choose a cereal color and then place his or her twelve pieces of cereal on the dark squares in the first three rows on his or her side of the game board. Explain that students are going to play a game similar to checkers. Have player A draw a word card and read it to player B. If player B correctly spells the word, he or she moves one "game piece" in a diagonal direction one space. If player B gives an incorrect response, player A correctly spells the word and places the word card at the bottom of the pile and player B's turn is over. When a player "jumps over" and captures an opponent's game piece, he or she should remove that piece from the game board. Have students continue to take turns spelling words until one player has captured all of his or her partner's cereal pieces.

Vv
variation

Write antonyms or synonyms on the index cards. Challenge students to say a matching antonym or synonym of the word in order to move a game piece.

Fruity Checkers

Making Your Word Wall More Interactive © 2001 Creative Teaching Press

Word Race

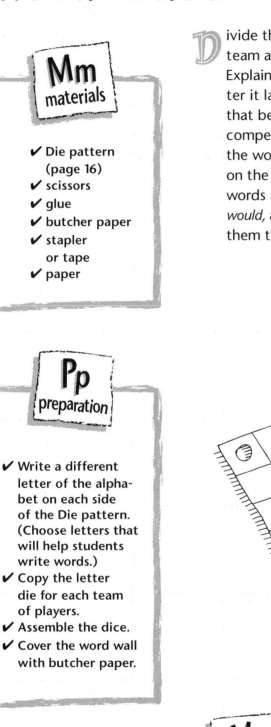

Mm
materials

✔ Die pattern
  (page 16)
✔ scissors
✔ glue
✔ butcher paper
✔ stapler
  or tape
✔ paper

Pp
preparation

✔ Write a different
  letter of the alpha-
  bet on each side
  of the Die pattern.
  (Choose letters that
  will help students
  write words.)
✔ Copy the letter
  die for each team
  of players.
✔ Assemble the dice.
✔ Cover the word wall
  with butcher paper.

ivide the class into teams of two to four players. Give each team a letter die, and give each player a piece of paper. Explain that one player will roll the die and announce the letter it lands on. Each team member will write word wall words that begin with that letter. Then, the team members will compete to write words that have the same phonogram as the word wall words they listed. For example, if the die lands on the letter *c*, team members might write the word wall words *cat* and *could*. Then, they might write *mat, flat, bat, would,* and *should*. Have players count their words and read them to each other.

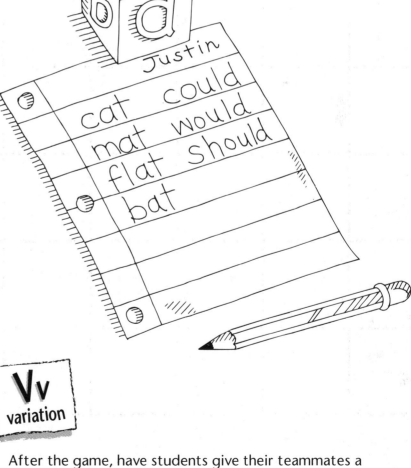

Vv
variation

After the game, have students give their teammates a spelling quiz using the words they wrote.

Word Wall Words in Stories

ivide the class into teams of two to four students. Give each team a piece of writing paper. Explain that each team is going to write a creative story that makes sense, using as many word wall words as possible. Tell students their team earns a point for each word wall word. Make it clear that each team member must contribute to the writing of the story even though each team will only turn in one paper. Tell students their story must have a title. Explain that they can add a prefix or suffix to any word wall word and still count it at the end of the activity. Encourage students to look at the word wall to help with spelling. Have teams revise and edit their finished stories. Have each team underline and count all of their word wall words. Ask a team member to write the total number of underlined words on the top corner of their paper. The team with the most underlined words wins the game.

Mm
materials

✔ writing paper

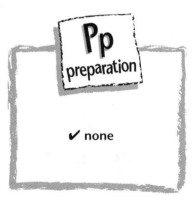

Pp
preparation

✔ none

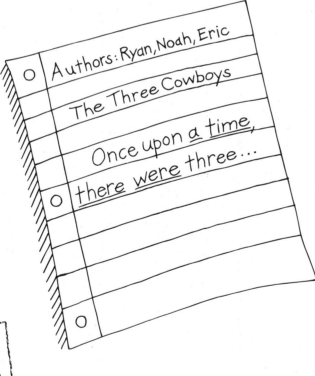

Vv
variation

Have teams share their story with the class. Have the class clap each time they hear a word wall word. Invite students to illustrate the stories.

Crisscross Words

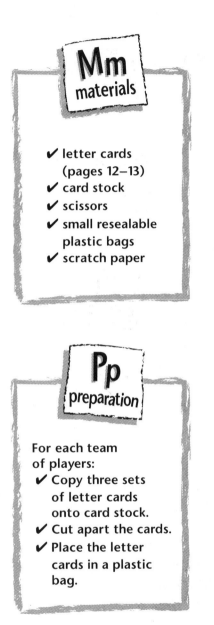

Mm materials

- ✔ letter cards (pages 12–13)
- ✔ card stock
- ✔ scissors
- ✔ small resealable plastic bags
- ✔ scratch paper

Pp preparation

For each team of players:
- ✔ Copy three sets of letter cards onto card stock.
- ✔ Cut apart the cards.
- ✔ Place the letter cards in a plastic bag.

ivide the class into teams of three to four players. Explain that students will be playing a game similar to Scrabble®. Give each team a bag of letters and a piece of scratch paper. Have teams spread out their cards facedown on the table. Invite each player to choose seven cards and place them face-up on the table. Have the first player on each team use his or her cards to spell a word wall word and then place the cards in a row on the table. Tell the player to draw the same number of new cards as cards used and then record on the scratch paper one point for each letter in his or her word. If players cannot spell a word wall word with their cards, allow them to exchange any number of their cards for new ones. Remind players that they cannot move or remove any cards once they have been placed on the table. The game is over when no player can create any new words or when one player uses his or her last card. Have players tally their points to determine who won the game.

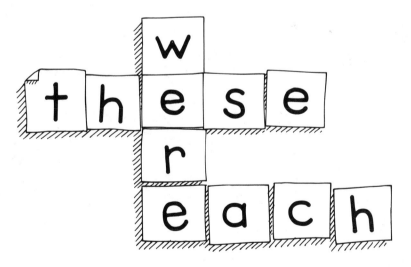

Vv variation

Have students use words with the same phonogram as words from the word wall.

Stack Them Up

ivide the class into teams of two to four players. Give each team a set of word cards, a die, and 20 building blocks. Have the first player on each team roll the die. Ask the second player to select that number of cards and read each word to the first player. Invite the first player to spell each word. Have the first player take a block for each word he or she spelled correctly and use the blocks to begin building a tower. Invite players to continue taking turns spelling words until all the blocks are used. The player who builds the tallest tower wins the game.

Mm
materials

✔ index cards
✔ dice
✔ building blocks

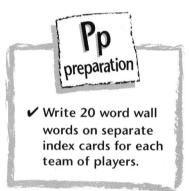

Pp
preparation

✔ Write 20 word wall words on separate index cards for each team of players.

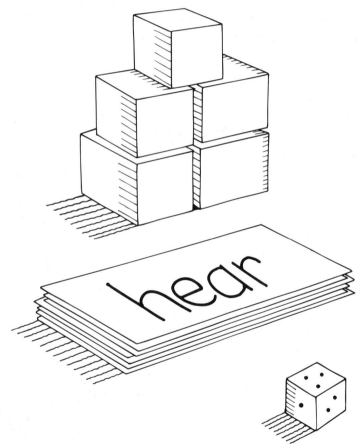

Vv
variation

Have each student begin with a completed tower and remove a block for each word he or she spelled correctly. The first student to remove all of his or her blocks wins the game.

No More Fish

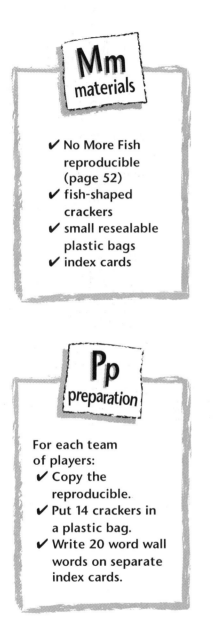

Mm materials

✔ No More Fish reproducible (page 52)
✔ fish-shaped crackers
✔ small resealable plastic bags
✔ index cards

Pp preparation

For each team of players:
✔ Copy the reproducible.
✔ Put 14 crackers in a plastic bag.
✔ Write 20 word wall words on separate index cards.

Divide the class into teams of two to three players. Give each team a reproducible, a bag of crackers, and a set of word wall cards. Explain that the object of the game is to be the last player to pick up a fish cracker. Ask a team member to place the crackers on the game board. Invite players to take turns choosing the number of words (one or two) they will try to spell. Have a different team member select that number of cards and read aloud the word or words. Invite the player to remove a fish from the game board for each word he or she spells correctly. If the player misspells one or both words, he or she cannot remove any fish. Have players continue to take turns spelling words and removing fish until a player wins the game.

Vv variation

Have teams start without any fish on their game boards. Have students place on the board a fish for each word they spell correctly. The student who places the last fish wins the game.

No More Fish

Four Boxes in a Row

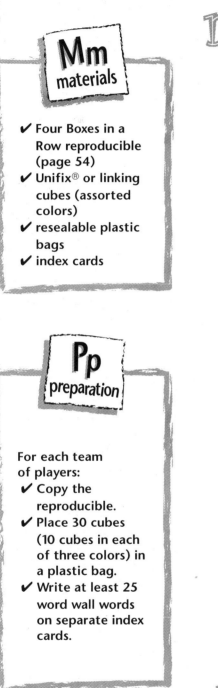

Mm
materials

- ✔ Four Boxes in a Row reproducible (page 54)
- ✔ Unifix® or linking cubes (assorted colors)
- ✔ resealable plastic bags
- ✔ index cards

Pp
preparation

For each team of players:
- ✔ Copy the reproducible.
- ✔ Place 30 cubes (10 cubes in each of three colors) in a plastic bag.
- ✔ Write at least 25 word wall words on separate index cards.

Divide the class into teams of two to three players. Give each team a reproducible, a bag of cubes, and a set of word cards. Have teams place the cards facedown in a pile. Invite each player to choose a cube color. Explain that the object of the game is to be the first player to place four cubes in a row (horizontally, vertically, or diagonally) on the game board. Have a player pick the top card from the pile and read the word for the first player to spell. If the player correctly spells the word, have him or her place a cube on the game board. Have players continue to take turns spelling words and placing cubes on the board until a player wins the game.

Vv
variation

Have teams begin the game with their game board covered with cubes. The first student to remove four cubes in a row wins the game.

Four Boxes in a Row

Build a Bug

Mm
materials

✔ Build a Bug repro-
   ducible (page 56)
✔ card stock or
   construction paper
✔ scissors
✔ toothpicks
✔ small resealable
   plastic bags
✔ index cards
✔ dice

Pp
preparation

✔ Copy a class set
   of the reproducible
   onto card stock or
   construction paper.
✔ Laminate the copies.
   (optional)
✔ Cut 12 toothpicks in
   half, and place them
   in a plastic bag for
   each student.
✔ Write at least 30
   word wall words on
   separate index cards
   for each team of
   players.

ivide the class into teams of two to four players. Give each player a reproducible and a bag of toothpicks. Give each team a die and a set of word cards. Have teams place the cards facedown in a pile. Explain that the object of the game is to be the first player to complete his or her "bug." Have player A roll the die and player B choose that many word cards and read them to player A. Then, have player A spell the words. Invite player A to place a toothpick on his or her reproducible for each word he or she spelled correctly. Have players take turns spelling words until a player wins the game.

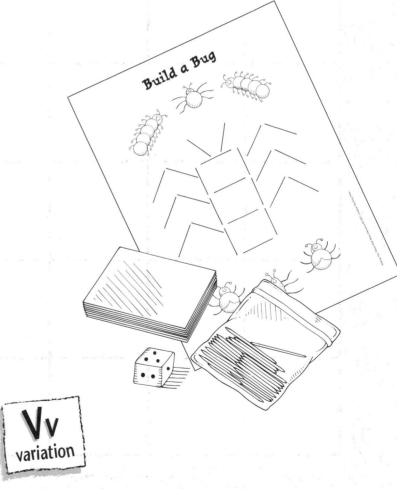

Vv
variation

Write *lose a turn* on three index cards and *place two free toothpicks on your bug* on two index cards. Give a set of these cards to each team to include with their word cards. If students choose a card without a word wall word on it, have them follow the directions on the card.

Build a Bug

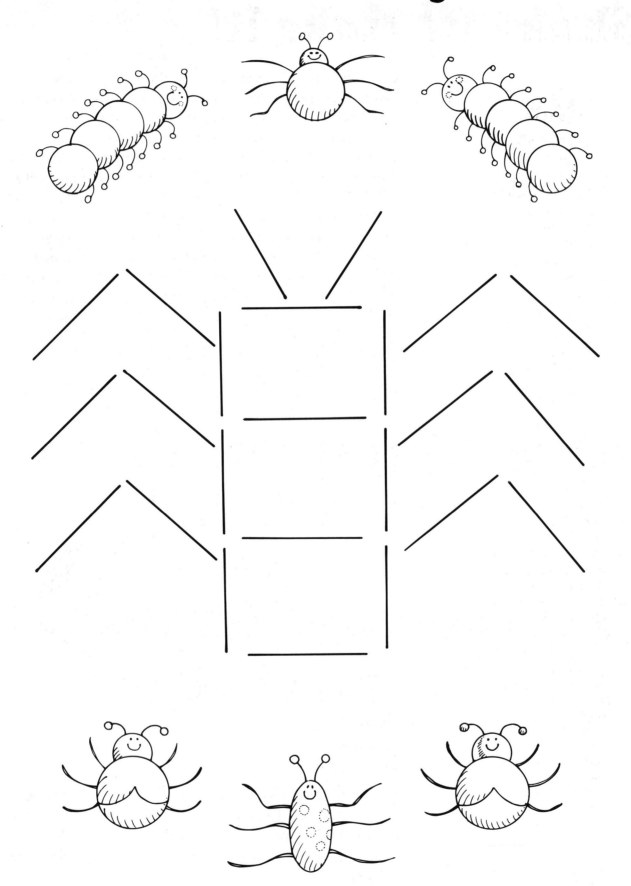

Making Your Word Wall More Interactive © 2001 Creative Teaching Press

Shake It! Make It!

Mm materials

✔ Shake It! Make It! reproducible (page 58)
✔ glue
✔ small shirt boxes
✔ beans
✔ index cards
✔ paper

Divide the class into teams of two to four players. Give each team a shirt box with a bean in it and a set of word cards. Give each player a piece of paper. Have teams place the cards facedown in a pile. Have the first player shake the box and open it to see which number the bean landed on. This is the number of words that the player must create. Then, invite him or her to pick a card and read the word on it. Encourage the player to name words from the same word family. For example, if the bean lands on 4 and the player chooses the word card *did,* he or she could write *hid, kid, lid,* and *middle.* Award the player a point for every word that he or she spelled correctly. Have players continue to take turns creating new words with the remaining cards. The player with the most points wins the game.

Pp preparation

For each team of players:
✔ Copy the reproducible.
✔ Glue the reproducible to the inside bottom of a shirt box.
✔ Place a bean in each box.
✔ Write on separate index cards 20 word wall words that have phonograms from which new words can easily be created. For example, students could create *fright, bright,* and *flight* from the word wall word *might.*

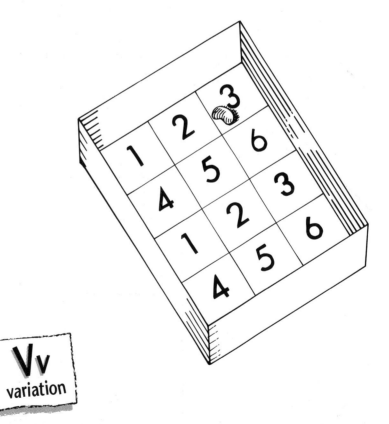

Vv variation

Instead of using shirt boxes, number small scraps of paper from 1 to 6. Fold the papers in half, and place them in a small brown bag. Prepare a bag for each team. Invite students to randomly choose a number from the bag and complete the activity.

Shake It! Make It!

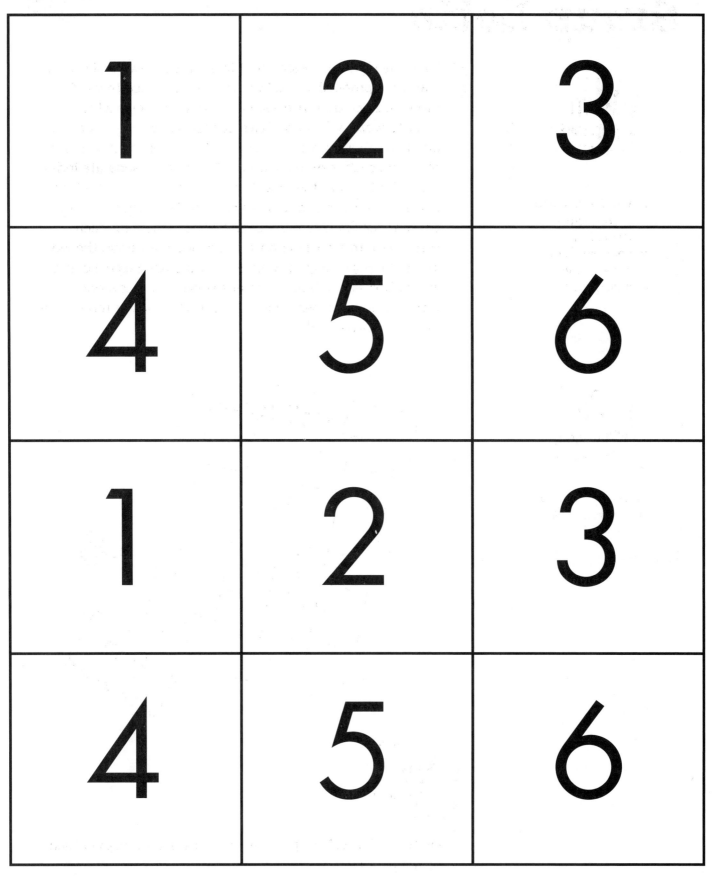

1	2	3
4	5	6
1	2	3
4	5	6

58

Making Your Word Wall More Interactive © 2001 Creative Teaching Press

Group Lotto

Mm
materials

✔ Word Wall Lotto
  reproducible
  (page 24)
✔ counters (e.g.,
  cubes, beans)
✔ index cards

Pp
preparation

✔ Copy a class set of
  the reproducible.

D ivide the class into teams of at least three players. Give each player a reproducible and 16 counters. Give each team 16 blank index cards. Invite each team to brainstorm a list of 16 favorite word wall words. Have each player on the team randomly write a word in each box on his or her sheet. Ask one player on each team to write the 16 words on separate index cards. Explain that the object of the game is to be the first player to cover four words in a row (horizontally, vertically, or diagonally). Invite a player to be the "caller" for each team. Have this player choose a card and read aloud the word. Invite the other players to spell the word and place a counter in that box. Have players continue spelling and covering words until one player wins the game. Have teams repeat the game with a new caller.

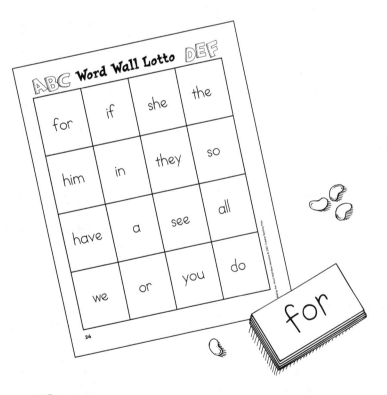

Vv
variation

Invite the "caller" to spell the words instead of reading them to the players.

Roll Off

D ivide the class into teams of two to four players. Give each player a reproducible. Give each team a die and a set of word cards. Have teams place the cards facedown in a pile. Explain that the object of the game is to spell words and be the first player to fill in his or her game board. Have the first player roll the die. Ask another player to pick that number of word cards and read each word to the first player to spell. If the player correctly spells all the words, have him or her write the words on the lines next to the number rolled. If the player misspells any of the words, he or she cannot write any words. (If a player rolls a number more than once and has already completed that line, he or she loses a turn.) Have players continue rolling the die and spelling words until one player wins the game.

Mm materials

✔ Roll Off reproducible (page 61)
✔ Die pattern (page 16)
✔ scissors
✔ glue
✔ index cards

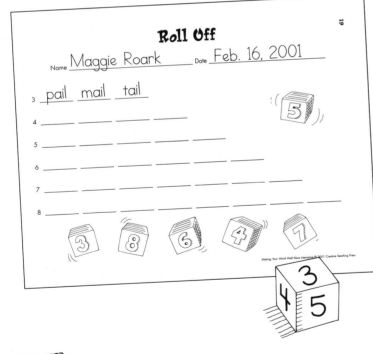

Pp preparation

✔ Copy a class set of the reproducible.
✔ Number the Die pattern from 3 to 8.
✔ Copy the die for each team of players.
✔ Assemble the dice.
✔ Write 30 word wall words on separate index cards for each team.

Vv variation

Write compound words, antonyms, synonyms, or homophones on the index cards.

Roll Off

Name _____ Date _____

3 _____

4 _____

5 _____

6 _____

7 _____

8 _____

Build a Sun

ivide the class into teams of two to four players. Give each player ten paper strips and one circle. Give each team a set of word cards. Have teams place the cards facedown in a pile. Explain that the object of the game is to be the first player to build a sun with ten rays. Have players place their "sun" (circle) in front of them. Ask a player to pick a card and read the word to the first player to spell. If the first player correctly spells the word, invite him or her to place a "ray" (strip) on his or her sun. If the first player misspells the word, he or she loses a turn and the teammate reads the correct spelling. Have players continue to take turns spelling words and adding rays to their sun until a player wins the game.

Mm materials

✔ yellow construction paper
✔ scissors
✔ index cards

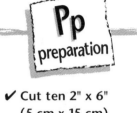

Pp preparation

✔ Cut ten 2" x 6" (5 cm x 15 cm) construction paper strips for each student.
✔ Cut out a 6" (15 cm) diameter construction paper circle for each student.
✔ Write at least 30 word wall words on separate index cards for each team of players.

Vv variation

Invite students to write the words they spell correctly on their rays.

62

Pick a Letter, Any Letter

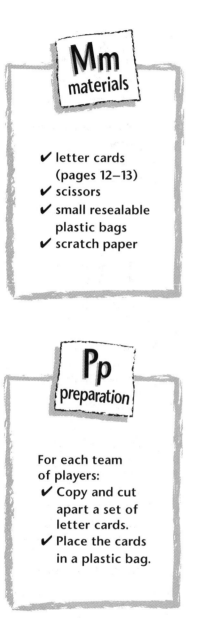

Mm materials

✔ letter cards (pages 12–13)
✔ scissors
✔ small resealable plastic bags
✔ scratch paper

Pp preparation

For each team of players:
✔ Copy and cut apart a set of letter cards.
✔ Place the cards in a plastic bag.

Divide the class into teams of two to four players. Give each team a bag of letters and a piece of scratch paper. Have players write their name on the paper. Explain that the object of the game is to earn the most points by spelling words. Invite the first player to take one letter card out of the bag. Ask a teammate to choose a word from the word wall that begins with the same letter as the letter card, and ask the first player to spell that word. (Encourage players to also choose words with the same phonograms as the word wall words for their teammates to spell.) If the first player correctly spells the word, have him or her mark on the scratch paper a point for each letter in the word. Ask the player to place the letter card back in the bag. Have players continue to take turns drawing letters and spelling words until a player wins the game.

Vv variation

Give each team a list of words. Have a student choose a word from the list that begins with the same letter as the letter card. Then, encourage another student to spell that word.

63

Bean Soup

ivide the class into teams of two to four players. Give each player a "soup" bowl, 20 beans, and a piece of scratch paper. Give each team a set of word cards. Have teams place the cards facedown in a pile. Explain that the object of the game is to be the first player to put 20 beans in his or her bowl. Have the first player pick a card from the pile and then, in 10 seconds, write as many words as possible from the same word family as the word on the card. (Ask the player's team-mates to hold up one finger at a time to count 10 seconds.) For example, if a player draws the word *about,* he or she could write *shout, out, pout, without, spout,* and *trout.* Walk around the class and randomly check players' papers. Invite the first player to place a bean in his or her bowl for each word he or she spelled correctly. Have players continue to take turns picking cards and writing words until a player wins the game.

Mm
materials

✔ index cards
✔ paper or plastic bowls
✔ beans
✔ scratch paper

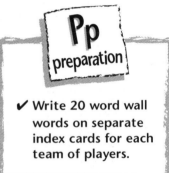

Pp
preparation

✔ Write 20 word wall words on separate index cards for each team of players.

Vv
variation

Have students start with 20 beans in their bowl. Invite them to remove a bean for every word they write that has the same phonogram as the word they picked from the pile. The first student to empty his or her bowl wins the game.

Find the Match

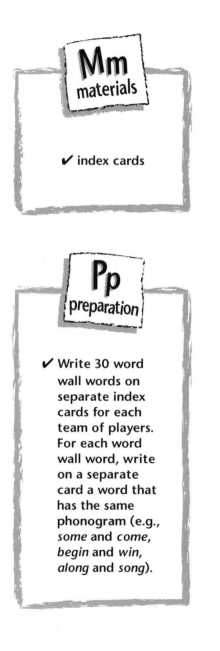

Mm
materials

✔ index cards

Pp
preparation

✔ Write 30 word wall words on separate index cards for each team of players. For each word wall word, write on a separate card a word that has the same phonogram (e.g., *some* and *come*, *begin* and *win*, *along* and *song*).

D ivide the class into teams of two to four players. Give each team a set of word cards. Explain that teams are going to play a game similar to Go Fish. Invite one player on each team to shuffle the cards, pass out six cards to each player, and place the remaining cards facedown in a pile. Have the first player choose a teammate and ask if that player has a word with the same phonogram as one of his or her words. For example, player A asks player B *Do you have a word from the same word family as the word* **come***?* Player B has the word *some* and gives player A that card. Player A places the two cards on the table. When a player does not have a word with a matching phonogram, the player whose turn it is chooses a card from the top of the pile. Have players continue taking turns until all the cards have been drawn. Have players count their matches. The player with the most matches wins the game.

Vv
variation

Create sets of antonym, synonym, compound word, or contraction word cards.

Cups of Words

Mm
materials

✔ small scraps of paper
✔ paper or plastic cups
✔ scratch paper

ave students work in pairs. Give each pair ten cups, ten scraps of folded paper, and a piece of scratch paper. Have students place each scrap of paper in a separate cup and turn the cups upside down. Explain that the number on the cup indicates how many words they will need to write and the word on the scrap paper indicates the word family they will use to create new words. Have one partner choose a cup, read the word on the scrap paper, and write new words. For example, if a student chooses the cup marked 4, which contains a scrap paper with the word *small,* he or she could write *mall, call, all,* and *tall.* Have students record on their paper a point for each word they spelled correctly. Have the student remove the cup and invite his or her partner to repeat the activity. Have partners continue in this manner with the remaining cups. The student with the most points wins the game.

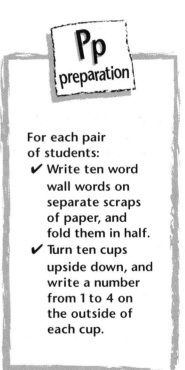

Pp
preparation

For each pair of students:
✔ Write ten word wall words on separate scraps of paper, and fold them in half.
✔ Turn ten cups upside down, and write a number from 1 to 4 on the outside of each cup.

Vv
variation

Have students build onto the words on the scraps of paper by adding a prefix or suffix (e.g., *small* becomes *smaller* and *smallest*).

Guess My Word

Mm materials

✔ index cards
✔ scratch paper

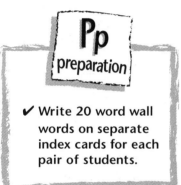

Pp preparation

✔ Write 20 word wall words on separate index cards for each pair of students.

Have students work in pairs. Give each pair a set of word cards and a piece of scratch paper. Invite one of the partners to shuffle the cards, deal five cards to both players, and then place the remaining cards facedown in a pile. Have player A draw a card (e.g., *because*) and give player B a clue about the word (e.g., *It begins with the letter b*). Ask player B to try to guess the word and spell it. If player B correctly spells the word based on one clue, have him or her record five points on the scratch paper. If player B cannot guess or spell the word, invite player A to give another clue. If player B has not guessed and spelled the word after five clues, ask player A to read aloud the word, and have player B try to spell it to earn one point. Have players take turns giving clues and trying to guess and spell words with the remaining cards. The player with the most points wins the game.

Vv variation

Have partners compete against other partners. Have the two sets of partners take turns giving clues to each other. The pair with the most points wins the game.

Letters in My First Name

Name _____

Date _____

Directions: Write each letter of your first name on a separate line in the first column. Find as many words as you can from the word wall that begin with each letter of your first name and write them on the lines in the same row. If you find more than four words, choose the four you would like to write. If a letter appears in your name more than once and you have already used all the word wall words, write other words that begin with the same letter.

Letters in My First Name   Word Wall Words

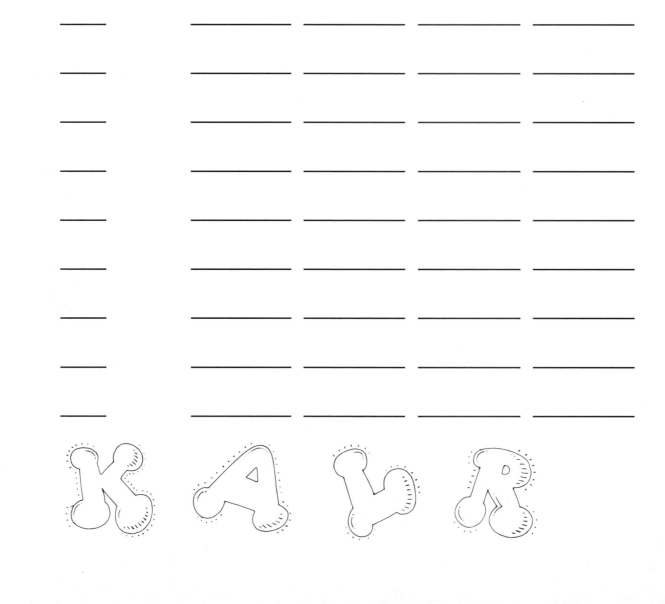

Making Your Word Wall More Interactive © 2001 Creative Teaching Press

Letters in My Last Name

Name _____

Date _____

Directions: Write each letter of your last name on a separate line in the first column. Find as many words as you can from the word wall that begin with each letter of your last name and write them on the lines in the same row. If you find more than four words, choose the four you would like to write. If a letter appears in your name more than once and you have already used all the word wall words, write other words that begin with the same letter.

Letters in My Last Name   Word Wall Words

____   _____   _____   _____   _____

____   _____   _____   _____   _____

____   _____   _____   _____   _____

____   _____   _____   _____   _____

____   _____   _____   _____   _____

____   _____   _____   _____   _____

____   _____   _____   _____   _____

____   _____   _____   _____   _____

____   _____   _____   _____   _____

Letters in Words

Name _____

Date _____

Directions: Write ten word wall words in the first column. Find two more words on the word wall that have the same number of letters as the first word. Write these words in the boxes next to your word wall words.

Word Wall Words   Other Word Wall Words with the Same Number of Letters

Making Your Word Wall More Interactive © 2001 Creative Teaching Press

How Much Are Words Worth?

Name _____

Date _____

Directions: Search the word wall for words that add up to the same "value" as the numbers in the *Word Values* column. Use the Letter Bank to find the value of each letter. Record your findings.

```
                        Letter Bank

    a = 1    b = 2    c = 3    d = 2    e = 1    f = 2
    g = 3    h = 2    i = 2    j = 1    k = 1    l = 2
    m = 2    n = 2    o = 1    p = 3    q = 2    r = 1
    s = 2    t = 2    u = 1    v = 2    w = 1    x = 1
    y = 1    z = 5
```

Word Values   Word Wall Words with the Same Value

Word Values	Word Wall Words with the Same Value
5	
5	
6	
6	
7	
7	
8	
8	
9	
10	

Making Your Word Wall More Interactive © 2001 Creative Teaching Press

Syllables in Words

Name _____

Date _____

Directions: Write ten word wall words in the first column. Write the number of syllables in each word in the second column. Answer the questions at the bottom of the page.

Word Wall Words   How Many Syllables?

_____   _____

_____   _____

_____   _____

_____   _____

_____   _____

_____   _____

_____   _____

_____   _____

_____   _____

_____   _____

be-cause   *Sail-boat*   *a-bout*   *like*

Which word has the largest number of syllables? _____

Which word has the smallest number of syllables? _____

Which words have the same number of syllables? _____

72

Words in ABC Order

Name _____

Date _____

Directions: Write ten word wall words in the first column. Arrange the words in alphabetical order in the second column. Finish the sentence at the bottom of the page.

Word Wall Words   Words in Alphabetical Order

_____   _____

_____   _____

_____   _____

_____   _____

_____   _____

_____   _____

_____   _____

_____   _____

_____   _____

_____   _____

My words range from the letter _____ to the letter _____.

The Shape of Words

Name _____

Date _____

Directions: Write ten word wall words in the first column. Count and record the number of tall, small, and dropped letters in each word. Answer the questions at the bottom of the page.

Word Wall Words	Number of Tall Letters	Number of Small Letters	Number of Dropped Letters
_____	_____	_____	_____
_____	_____	_____	_____
_____	_____	_____	_____
_____	_____	_____	_____
_____	_____	_____	_____
_____	_____	_____	_____
_____	_____	_____	_____
_____	_____	_____	_____
_____	_____	_____	_____

The word with the most tall letters is _____.

The word with the most small letters is _____.

The word with the most dropped letters is _____.

Making Your Word Wall More Interactive © 2001 Creative Teaching Press

Vowels and Consonants in Words

Name _____

Date _____

Directions: Write ten word wall words in the first column. Count the number of vowels in each word and write that number in the second column. Count the number of consonants in each word and write that number in the third column. Add up the two numbers and write the total number of letters in the last column.

Word Wall Words	Number of Vowels	+	Number of Consonants	=	Total Number of Letters
_____	_____		_____		_____
_____	_____		_____		_____
_____	_____		_____		_____
_____	_____		_____		_____
_____	_____		_____		_____
_____	_____		_____		_____
_____	_____		_____		_____
_____	_____		_____		_____
_____	_____		_____		_____
_____	_____		_____		_____

What Fraction Are Vowels?

Name _____

Date _____

Directions: Write ten word wall words in the first column. Count the letters in each word and write that number in the *Total Letters* column. Then, count the number of vowels in the word and write that number in the *Vowels* column. Finally, write the "vowel fraction" in the last column. For example, two out of five letters in the word *where* are vowels, so the fraction is ²/₅.

Word Wall Words	Total Letters	Vowels	Vowel Fraction
_____	_____	_____	_____
_____	_____	_____	_____
_____	_____	_____	_____
_____	_____	_____	_____
_____	_____	_____	_____
_____	_____	_____	_____
_____	_____	_____	_____
_____	_____	_____	_____
_____	_____	_____	_____
_____	_____	_____	_____

Making Your Word Wall More Interactive © 2001 Creative Teaching Press

What Fraction Are Consonants?

Name _____

Date _____

Directions: Write ten word wall words in the first column. Count the letters in each word and write that number in the *Total Letters* column. Then, count the number of consonants in the word and write that number in the *Consonants* column. Finally, write the "consonant fraction" in the last column. For example, three out of five letters in the word *where* are consonants, so the fraction is $^3/_5$.

Word Wall Words	Total Letters	Consonants	Consonant Fraction
_____	_____	_____	_____
_____	_____	_____	_____
_____	_____	_____	_____
_____	_____	_____	_____
_____	_____	_____	_____
_____	_____	_____	_____
_____	_____	_____	_____
_____	_____	_____	_____
_____	_____	_____	_____
_____	_____	_____	_____

Making Twenty

Name _____

Date _____

Directions: Write a word wall word in each box. Write under each box new words from the same word family. Underline the part of each word that has the same letters as the other words in the group. Complete the sentence at the bottom of the page.

☐	☐
1._____	1._____
2._____	2._____
3._____	3._____
4._____	4._____
☐	☐
1._____	1._____
2._____	2._____
3._____	3._____
4._____	4._____

The parts of words I underlined are

_____, _____, _____, _____.

Making Your Word Wall More Interactive © 2001 Creative Teaching Press

I Can Spell

Name _____

Date _____

Directions: Write ten word wall words in the first column. In the second column, write words from the same word family as the words in the first column. Complete the sentence at the bottom of the page.

If I know this word:	Then I can spell this new word:

My favorite word wall word is _____ because _____

_____.

Let's Be Creative

Directions: Write a creative story using as many word wall words as you can. Underline each word wall word you use.

Title: _____

Author: _____

_____

_____

_____

_____

_____

_____

_____

_____

_____

Total number of word wall words I used in my story: _____

Making Your Word Wall More Interactive © 2001 Creative Teaching Press

Graphing My Favorite Word

Name _____

Date _____

Directions: Choose ten of your favorite word wall words. Write each word in a box in the first column of the graph. Show five to ten classmates the words. Ask each classmate to choose his or her favorite word from your list and write it in the same row.

Word	1	2	3	4	5

Which word was chosen the most? _____

Which word was chosen the least? _____

Write one thing you learned from your graph. _____

_____

Be the Teacher!

Directions: Write ten words from the word wall in the first column to create a spelling quiz for a classmate. Read each word to your classmate. Write the word on the line in the second column as your classmate spells it to you. Compare the spelling of the words. Give your classmate a score at the bottom of the page.

This quiz was created by _____.

This quiz was given to _____.

Word Wall Words	My Classmate's Spelling of the Word Wall Words
1._____	1._____
2._____	2._____
3._____	3._____
4._____	4._____
5._____	5._____
6._____	6._____
7._____	7._____
8._____	8._____
9._____	9._____
10._____	10._____

My classmate's score ☐

I ♥ MY TEACHER

Making Your Word Wall More Interactive © 2001 Creative Teaching Press

Word Wall Probability

Mm
materials

✔ Word Wall Probability reproducible (page 84)
✔ Word Wall Probability Record Sheet (page 85)
✔ small slips of paper
✔ small paper bags

Pp
preparation

✔ Copy the reproducible and the record sheet for each student.

iscuss the term *probability* with students prior to having them complete this activity. Give each student the two reproducibles, ten slips of paper, and one small paper bag. Invite students to use the reproducibles to complete the activity.

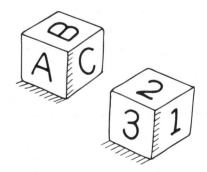

Grid Words

Mm
materials

✔ Grid Words reproducible (page 86)
✔ Grid Words Record Sheet (page 87)
✔ Die pattern (page 16)
✔ scissors
✔ glue

Pp
preparation

✔ Copy the reproducible and the record sheet for each student.
✔ Label four sides of one Die pattern with the numerals 1, 2, 3, and 4. Write any numerals from 1 to 4 on the remaining sides.
✔ Label four sides of a second Die pattern with the letters A, B, C, and D. Write any letters from A to D on the remaining sides.
✔ Make a copy of each die for each student.
✔ Assemble the dice.

ive each student the two reproducibles and a set of dice. Invite students to use the reproducibles and dice to complete the activity.

Word Wall Probability

1. Choose ten words from the word wall. Write each word on a slip of paper and place the slips of paper in your bag.

2. Write the same ten words in the first column of your Word Wall Probability Record Sheet.

3. Predict which word you will pick the most and write your prediction at the top of your record sheet.

4. Shake your bag and, without looking, take out one slip of paper.

5. Read the word you picked.

6. Use tally marks to record your results on your record sheet.

7. Place the slip of paper back in the bag.

8. Repeat steps four to seven 19 times.

9. Answer the questions at the bottom of your record sheet.

Making Your Word Wall More Interactive © 2001 Creative Teaching Press

Word Wall Probability Record Sheet

Name _____

Date _____

Predict which word will be picked most. _____

Why did you choose this word? _____

My Word Wall Words   Tally Marks

_____   _____

_____   _____

_____   _____

_____   _____

_____   _____

_____   _____

_____   _____

_____   _____

_____   _____

Which word was picked most? _____

Which word was picked least? _____

Which words were not picked? _____

Grid Words

1. Choose 16 words from the word wall. Write each word in a box on your Grid Words Record Sheet.

2. Roll the number and letter dice together.

3. Find the word in the box with the same coordinates.

4. Record the word at the bottom of your record sheet.

5. Repeat steps two to four 9 times.

Grid Words Record Sheet

Name Scotty Robinson

Date March 10, 2001

	A	B	C	D
4	student	leg	horse	shirt
				frame
3	where	house	plant	
			note	jump
2	great	smile		weed
			dress	
1	could	bank		

Words I Rolled

1. _____
2. _____

6. _____
7. _____
8. _____
9. _____

Making Your Word Wall More Interactive © 2001 Creative Teaching Press

Grid Words Record Sheet

Name _____

Date _____

	A	B	C	D
4				
3				
2				
1				

Words I Rolled

1. _____
2. _____
3. _____
4. _____
5. _____

6. _____
7. _____
8. _____
9. _____
10. _____

Making Your Word Wall More Interactive © 2001 Creative Teaching Press

Word Wall Spelling Quiz

Name _____

Date _____

1. _____

2. _____

3. _____

4. _____

5. _____

6. _____

7. _____

8. _____

9. _____

10. _____

11. _____

12. _____

13. _____

14. _____

15. _____

16. _____

17. _____

18. _____

19. _____

20. _____

My Portable Word Wall

Name _____

Date _____

Aa	Bb	Cc	Dd
Ee	Ff	Gg	Hh
Ii	Jj	Kk	Ll

My Portable Word Wall

Name _____

Date _____

High-Frequency Words

Mm	Nn	Oo	Pp
Qq	Rr	Ss	Tt
Uu	Vv	Ww	Xx, Yy, Zz

High-Frequency Words

a	each	into	or	time
about	first	is	other	to
all	for	it	out	too
an	from	like	over	two
and	get	look	people	up
are	go	made	said	use
as	good	make	see	very
at	great	many	she	was
be	had	may	should	way
because	has	me	so	we
been	have	more	some	were
but	he	my	than	what
by	her	no	the	when
can	here	not	their	which
come	him	now	them	who
could	his	of	then	will
day	how	off	there	with
do	I	on	these	word
does	if	one	they	would
down	in	only	this	you

Compound Words

afternoon	cheeseburger	flagpole	ladybug	railroad
airline	classroom	flashlight	lifetime	rainbow
airport	cowboy	football	lighthouse	rattlesnake
anybody	cupcake	footprint	moonlight	rowboat
anyone	daytime	forever	motorcycle	sailboat
baseball	doorbell	goldfish	newspaper	sandbox
bathrobe	downhill	hairbrush	nobody	seashore
bedroom	downstairs	handshake	notebook	shipwreck
beside	dragonfly	homework	outdoors	shortstop
blackbird	drawstring	houseboat	outline	sunburn
blackboard	dugout	however	outside	surfboard
blackout	eardrum	icebox	pancake	textbook
breakfast	eggshell	inchworm	paperback	toothpick
broomstick	elsewhere	inside	password	tugboat
butterfly	everybody	into	peanut	underline
campfire	fingernail	jellyfish	peppermint	wastebasket
catfish	fireplace	junkyard	pigtail	without

Making Your Word Wall More Interactive © 2001 Creative Teaching Press

Antonyms

above/below	down/up	lose/win
alike/different	dry/wet	many/few
always/never	early/late	noisy/quiet
asleep/awake	easy/hard	on/off
back/front	empty/full	part/whole
beautiful/ugly	far/near	pull/push
before/after	fast/slow	rich/poor
begin/end	first/last	rough/smooth
best/worst	forget/remember	save/spend
bottom/top	give/take	short/tall
clean/dirty	happy/sad	start/stop
close/open	hard/soft	tame/wild
cold/hot	healthy/sick	thick/thin
crooked/straight	high/low	true/false
dark/light	large/small	usual/unusual
day/night	leave/stay	wide/narrow
deep/shallow	long/short	

Synonyms

above/over	end/finish	loud/noisy
afraid/scared	enormous/gigantic	mix/blend
answer/reply	false/untrue	mom/mother
automobile/car	fast/quick	need/require
begin/start	find/discover	nice/kind
below/under	forgive/excuse	promise/pledge
big/huge	gift/present	rip/tear
blank/empty	glad/happy	road/street
boat/ship	go/leave	say/tell
buy/purchase	hear/listen	sea/ocean
close/near	honest/sincere	small/tiny
correct/right	hurry/rush	talk/speak
dad/father	ill/sick	teach/instruct
desire/want	illustration/picture	tired/sleepy
dirty/filthy	jump/hop	whole/entire
easy/simple	keep/save	yell/scream
elect/choose	late/tardy	

Phonograms

-ack	-at	-ight	-op
-ail	-ate	-ill	-or
-ain	-aw	-in	-ore
-ake	-ay	-ine	-uck
-ale	-eat	-ing	-ug
-ame	-ell	-ink	-ump
-an	-est	-ip	-unk
-ank	-ice	-ir	
-ap	-ick	-ock	
-ash	-ide	-oke	

Homophones

ad/add	eye/I	in/inn
allowed/aloud	fair/fare	knot/not
ate/eight	find/fined	know/no
band/banned	flea/flee	loan/lone
bare/bear	flew/flu/flue	meat/meet
be/bee	for/fore/four	one/won
been/bin	genes/jeans	pail/pale
blew/blue	groan/grown	pair/pare/pear
board/bored	guessed/guest	peak/peek
buy/by	hair/hare	right/write
capital/capitol	halve/have	sail/sale
cent/scent/sent	hear/here	sea/see
Chile/chili/chilly	heard/herd	son/sun
close/clothes	hi/high	wait/weight
creak/creek	hire/higher	waste/waist
dear/deer	hole/whole	wood/would
desert/dessert	hour/our	

Making Your Word Wall More Interactive © 2001 Creative Teaching Press